BODY PARTS
身体部位
WITHDRAWN

Grow vocabulary by:

- **Looking** at pictures and words
- Talking about what you see
- **Touching** and naming objects
- **Using** questions to extend learning...
  Ask questions that invite children
  to share information.
  Begin your questions with words like...
  who, what, when, where and how.

Explanation:

1. Pīnyīn is the official Mandarin romanization system to pronounce Chinese characters.

2. Chinese pīnyīn romanization system uses four tones:
   - First tone: ā   high level
   - Second tone: á   rising
   - Third tone: ǎ   falling and then rising
   - Fourth tone: à   falling

3. The measure word may differ for each individual noun.

D1308051

These books support a series of educational games by Learning Props.
Learning Props, L.L.C., P.O. Box 774, Racine, WI 53401-0774
1-877-776-7750   www.learningprops.com

Created by: Bev Schumacher, Learning Props, L.L.C.
Graphic Design: Bev Kirk
Images: Hemera Technologies Inc., Matthew 25 Ministries, Bev Kirk, Jane Lund, Photos.com,
     123rf.com, Liquid Library

LEARNING *PROPS*

Library of Congress Control Number 2008907370   ISBN 978-1-935292-01-2

head
头

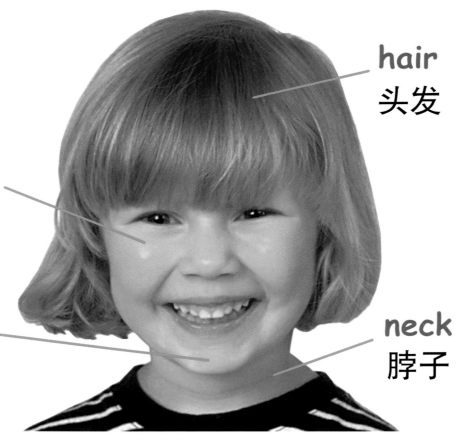

hair
头发

skin
皮肤

chin
下巴

neck
脖子

face
脸

forehead
额头

eye
眼睛

ear
耳朵

cheek
脸颊

nose
鼻子

mouth
嘴巴

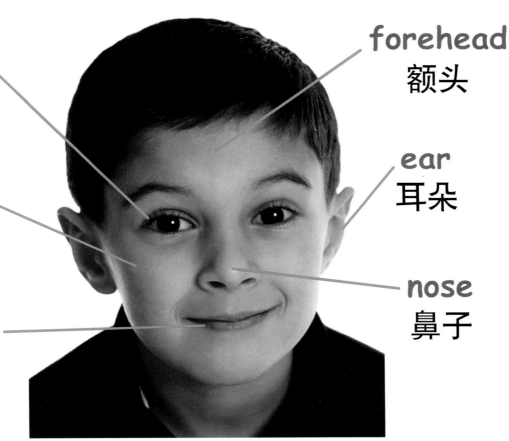

eye
眼睛

eyebrow
眉毛

eyelid
眼皮

eyelashes
睫毛

pupil
瞳孔

iris
虹膜

ear
耳朵

earlobe
耳垂

mouth
嘴巴

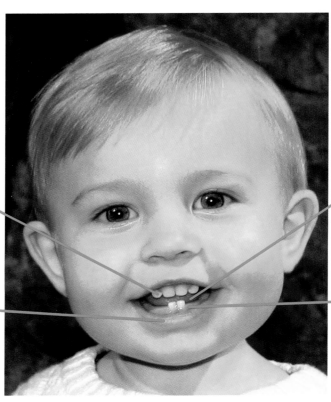

teeth
牙齿

tongue
舌头

lips
嘴唇

gums
牙龈

hair
头发

red hair

红头发

black hair

黑头发

blonde hair

金发

brown hair

棕发

straight hair

直发

curly hair

卷发

nose
鼻子

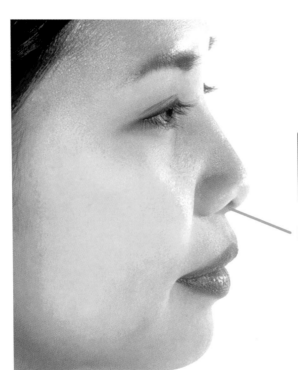

nostril
鼻孔

arm
手臂

hand
手

elbow
肘

shoulder
肩

wrist
手腕

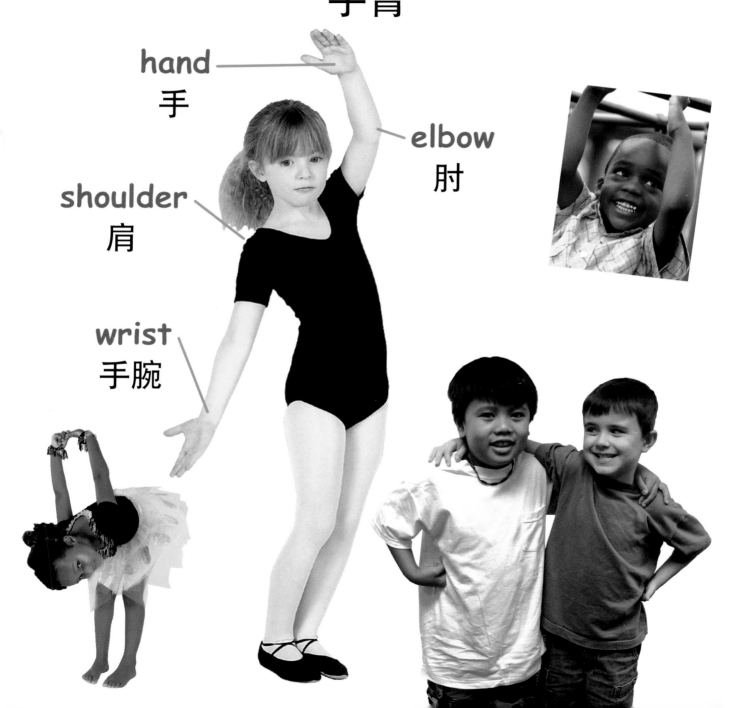

hand
手

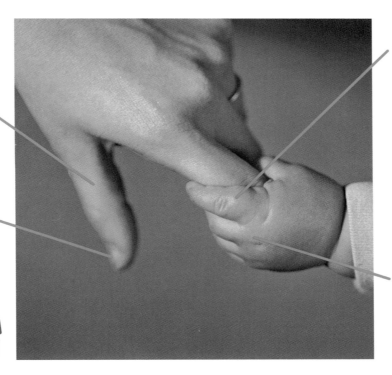

thumb
拇指

fingernail
指甲

palm
手掌

fingers
手指

knuckle
关节

leg
腿

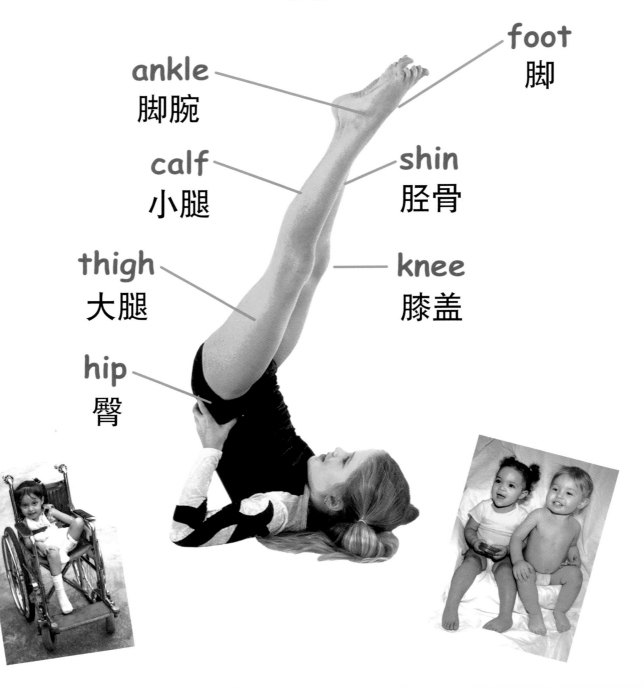

foot
脚

ankle
脚腕

shin
胫骨

calf
小腿

thigh
大腿

knee
膝盖

hip
臀

feet
脚

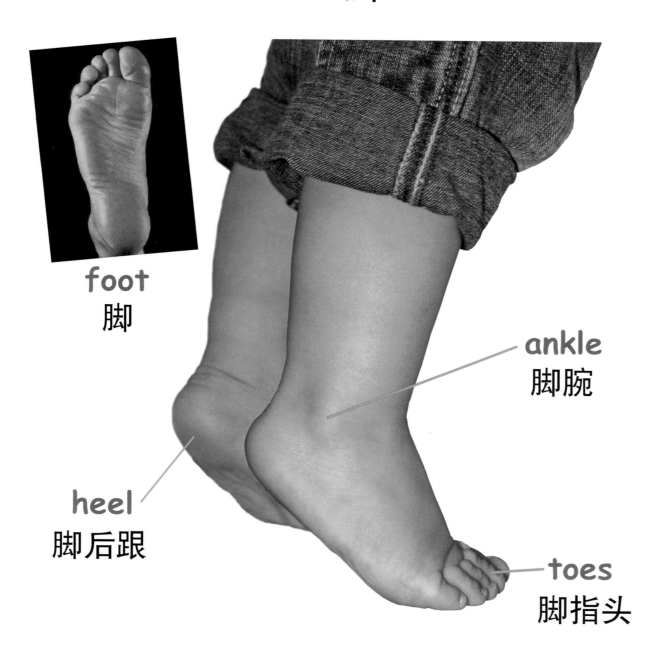

foot
脚

ankle
脚腕

heel
脚后跟

toes
脚指头

elbow
肘

shoulder
肩

stomach
肚子

chest
胸

hip
臀

waist
腰

chest
胸

back
背

bottom
屁股

Which body parts can you name?
你能叫出身体上哪部分的名称？

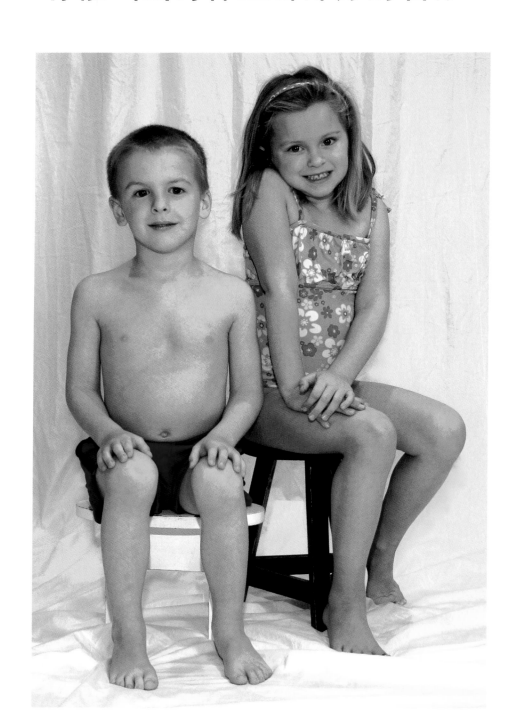

Which body parts can you name on these animals?
你能叫出这些动物身体上哪部分的名称？

pronunciation

Body Parts/**Bod**-ee **Parts**

Which body parts can you name?/
Wich bod-ee **parts kan yoo naym?**

Which body parts can you name on these animals?/
Wich bod-ee **parts kan yoo naym
on THeez an**-uh-muhlz?

pronunciation/pruh-*nuhn*-see-**ay**-shuhn

ankle/**ang**-kuhl
arm/**arm**
back/**bak**
bottom/**bot**-uhm
calf/kaf
cheek/**cheek**
chest/**chest**
chin/**chin**
ear/**ihr**
earlobe/**ihr**-loab
elbow/**el**-boh
eye/**eye**
eyebrow/**eye**-brou
eyelashes/**eye**-lash-es
eyelid/**eye**-lid
face/**fayss**
feet/**feet**
fingernail/**fing**-gur-nale
fingers/**fing**-gurs
foot/**fut**
forehead/**for**-hed
gums/**guhms**

hair/**hair**
   black hair/**blak hair**
   blonde hair/**blond hair**
   brown hair/**broun hair**
   curly hair/**kur**-lee **hair**
   red hair/**red hair**
   straight hair/**strayt hair**
hand/**hand**
head/**hed**
heel/**heel**
hip/**hip**
iris/**eye**-riss
knee/**nee**
knuckle/**nuhk**-uhl
leg/**leg**
lips/**lips**
mouth/**mouth**
neck/**nek**
nose/**nohz**
nostril/**noss**-truhl
palm/**pahm**
pupil/**pyoo**-puhl
shin/**shin**
shoulder/**shohl**-dur
skin/**skin**
stomach/**stuhm**-uhk
teeth/**teeTH**
thigh/**thye**
thumb/**thuhm**
toes/**tohs**
tongue/**tuhng**
waist/**wayst**
wrist/**rist**

pronunciation   发音

English / Chinese / Pīnyīn / Pronunciation

Body Parts / 身体部位 / shēn tǐ bù wèi / shun tee boo way

Which body parts can you name? / 你能叫出身体上哪部分的名称？ / nǐ néng jiào chū shēn tǐ shàng nǎ bù fēn de míng chēng?/ nee nuhng jyaow choo shun tee shahng nah boo fun duh meeng chun?

Which body parts can you name on these animals? / 你能叫出这些动物身体上哪部分的名称？ / nǐ néng jiào chū zhè xiē dòng wù shēn tǐ shàng nǎ bù fēn de míng chēng? / nee nuhng jyaow choo juh shyeh doong woo shun tee shahng nah boo fun duh meeng chun?

pronunciation / 发音 / fāyīn / fah een

ankle / 脚腕 / jiǎo wàn / jyaow wahn
arm / 手臂 / shǒu bì / show bee
back / 背 / bēi / bay
bottom / 屁股 / pì gu / pee goo
calf / 小腿 / xiǎo tuǐ / shyaow tway
cheek / 脸颊 / liǎn jiá / lyahn jyah
chest / 胸 / xiōng / shyoong
chin / 下巴 / xià ba / shyah bah
ear / 耳朵 / ěr duo / are dwaw
earlobe / 耳垂 / ěr chuí / are chway
elbow / 肘 / zhǒu / joe
eye / 眼睛 / yǎn jing / yan jeeng
eyebrow / 眉毛 / méi mao / may maow
eyelashes / 睫毛 / jié máo / jyeh maow
eyelid / 眼皮 / yǎn pí / yan pee
face / 脸 / liǎn / lyahn
feet / 脚 / jiǎo / jyaow
fingernail / 指甲 / zhǐ jiá / jir jyah
fingers / 手指 / shǒu zhǐ / show jir
foot / 脚 / jiǎo / jyaow
forehead / 额头 / é tóu / uh toe
gums / 牙龈 / yá yín / yah een
hair / 头发 / tóu fa / toe fah
  black hair / 黑头发 / hēi tóu fa / hay toe fah
  blonde hair / 金发 / jīn fa / jin fah
  brown hair / 棕发 / zōng fa / dzoong fah
  curly hair / 卷发 / juǎn fa / jwahn fah
  red hair / 红头发 / hóng tóu fa / hoong toe fah
  straight hair / 直发 / zhí fa / jir fah

hand / 手 / shǒu / show
head / 头 / tóu / toe
heel / 脚后跟 / jiǎo hòu gēn / jyaow hoe guhn
hip / 臀 / tún / twun
iris / 虹膜 / hóng mó / hoong maw
knee / 膝盖 / xī gài / she guy
knuckle / 关节 / guān jié / gwan jyeh
leg / 腿 / tuǐ / tway
lips / 嘴唇 / zuǐ chún / dzway chyew
mouth / 嘴巴 / zuǐ ba / dzway bah
neck / 脖子 / bó zi / baw dzuh
nose / 鼻子 / bí zi / bee dzuh
nostril / 鼻孔 / bí kǒng / bee koong
palm / 手掌 / shǒu zhǎng / show jahng
pupil / 瞳孔 / tóng kǒng / toong koong
shin / 胫骨 / jìng gǔ / jeeng goo
shoulder / 肩 / jiān / jyan
skin / 皮肤 / pí fū / pee foo
stomach / 肚子 / dǔ zi / doo dzuh
teeth / 牙齿 / yá chǐ / yah chir
thigh / 大腿 / dà tuǐ / dah tway
thumb / 拇指 / mǔ zhǐ / moo jir
toes / 脚指头 / jiǎo zhǐ tou / jyaow jir toe
tounge / 舌头 / shé tou/shuh toe
waist / 腰 / yāo / yaow
wrist / 手腕 / shǒu wàn / show wahn